RATS!

THE GOOD, THE BAD, AND THE UGLY

Richard Conniff

CROWN NEW YORK PUBLISHERS

A RAT IS BORN

One cold night in an underground burrow, a three-month-old rat stuffs a corner of her home with shredded rags, papers, and other soft material. Then she settles down on her nest and waits to give birth for the first time.

As her first pup is being born, she stirs it to life with a thorough licking. The pup is helpless. Its hairless flesh is pink as bubble gum. Its eyes and ears are sealed shut, and its legs are underdeveloped. But the struggle to survive starts now, because the pup soon has eleven brothers and sisters squirming together in the litter. They shove each other aside for a chance to nurse at Mom's nipples. A pup can grow fast enough to survive on its own after just four weeks—but only if it dives in and gets plenty of milk.

Young rats tag along with their mother at first. (Rat dads don't generally stay around to help with child-rearing.) They also play with their siblings, chasing, wrestling, and generally rehearsing to become adults. The youngsters soon strike out on their own, exploring new territories and sampling new foods.

Mom is probably too busy to notice. She mates again soon after giving birth, and she can deliver a new litter after a pregnancy of just twenty-two days. She may have sixty or seventy babies in a year. One type of domestic rat, the bandicoot in Asia, can produce a dozen litters and have fifteen thousand descendants (counting great-great-grandchildren) by the ripe old age of one year.

Five-day-old rat babies with Mom.

The youngsters
soon strike out
on their own.

Roof rat on a rope.

These buck-toothed, shortsighted riffraff are among our closest companions from the animal world. They live everywhere we do, often raiding our homes and stealing our food. Rats creep around at night and they spread disease. So they give most of us the willies. But in the medical laboratory, they also save lives by helping doctors find and test new treatments. And in some homes, a rat in a cage—or on a shoulder—is a treasured pet.

Rats belong to one of the most successful animal groups on earth, the rodents. Rodents have been around for more than 50 million years. The remains of one of the earliest specimens turned up in the fossilized droppings of an unknown predator, much as we still find rodent bones in owl pellets. Today, the scientific order Rodentia includes squirrels, mice, chipmunks, beavers—in fact, almost half of all mammal species. It also includes an appalling variety of rats, among them the noisy rat, the rajah rat, and the Namaqua rock rat.

But when people say, "Ugh, rats!" they're usually referring to the ones that attach themselves to human civilization. Scientists call them *commensal* rats, which literally means they share our table. There are two kinds of commensal rats in North America. The Norway rat (known to scientists as *Rattus norvegicus*) is bigger and more aggressive. The roof rat *(Rattus rattus),* now found mainly in the southern states and California, is smaller and, as the name suggests, a better climber.

In much of the world, these rats are relative newcomers. Roof rats first evolved somewhere in India. From there, they hitchhiked around the world with human travelers, becoming the first rats to reach Europe, as stowaways in ships carrying soldiers home from the Crusades. Despite their name, Norway rats actually originated in Manchuria, in what is now northeastern China. They reached Europe in about 1700 and sailed to North America with colonial settlers sometime after 1755.

Learning to live with humans is the smartest thing rats ever did. We've helped them become some of the most widely distributed animals on earth.

Norway, or brown, rat.

These buck-toothed riffraff are among our closest companions.

Roof, or black, rat.

9

WHAT BIG TEETH YOU HAVE AND OTHER BASIC BIOLOGY

People sometimes say they've seen a rat "as big as a cat." But the average Norway rat weighs less than a pound, roughly the size of an underfed squirrel, and measures no more than ten inches from tip of nose to base of tail. Roof rats are even smaller, typically weighing no more than twelve ounces.

Still, rats are impressive creatures. Like all rodents, they're built for gnawing. Their chisel-like front teeth grow constantly, up to five inches a year. The edges of uppers and lowers rub together, making the teeth self-sharpening and self-wearing (otherwise, we might have saber-toothed rats). A rat can use its teeth to gnaw through lead pipes, cinder blocks, or solid wood doors. It can bite with a force of twenty-four thousand pounds per square inch.

The rat's beady black eyes see poorly in daylight, but they're well suited to the night, allowing it to detect motion in dim light and even at a distance. The rat can hear sounds that are too high-pitched for us to hear and can smell things far better than we do. The rat also has catlike whiskers on its face and fine sensory hairs on its body, the better to feel its way along narrow passages. (Rats like to stay in contact with walls. They also avoid crossing open spaces. It's not because they're sneaky—it's because they're scared.) The rat's claws and the prominent pads on its feet help make it a skillful climber, and its long, naked tail provides support and balance. But the rat also uses its front feet the way we use our hands—for instance, to pick up its food.

Built for gnawing.

EYE

EAR

WHISKERS

FOOT

The rat's long, naked tail provides support and balance.

FOOT

TAIL

11

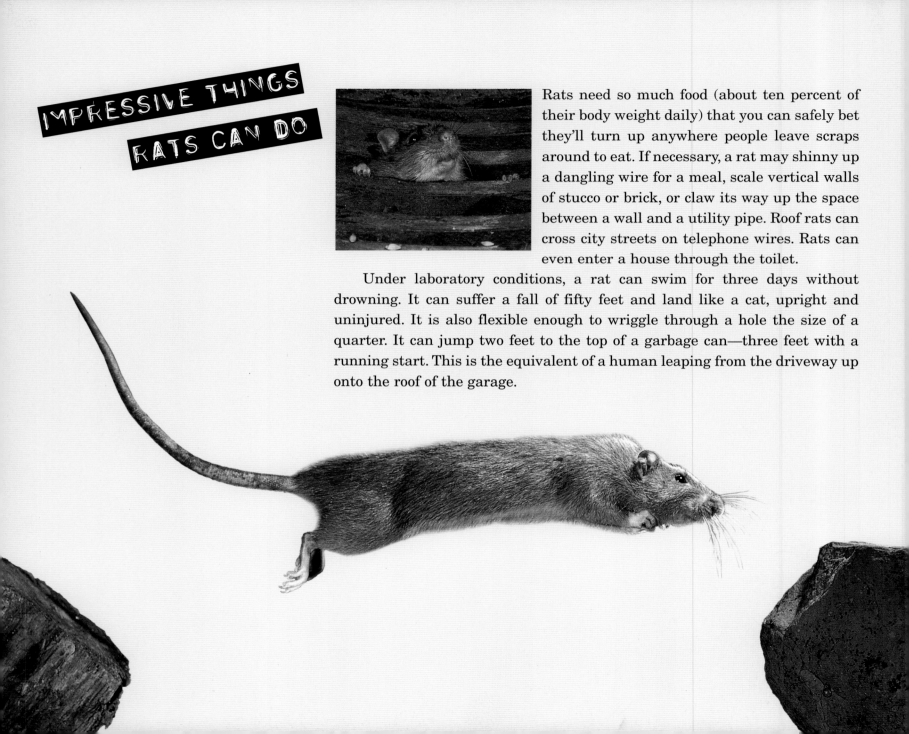

IMPRESSIVE THINGS RATS CAN DO

Rats need so much food (about ten percent of their body weight daily) that you can safely bet they'll turn up anywhere people leave scraps around to eat. If necessary, a rat may shinny up a dangling wire for a meal, scale vertical walls of stucco or brick, or claw its way up the space between a wall and a utility pipe. Roof rats can cross city streets on telephone wires. Rats can even enter a house through the toilet.

Under laboratory conditions, a rat can swim for three days without drowning. It can suffer a fall of fifty feet and land like a cat, upright and uninjured. It is also flexible enough to wriggle through a hole the size of a quarter. It can jump two feet to the top of a garbage can—three feet with a running start. This is the equivalent of a human leaping from the driveway up onto the roof of the garage.

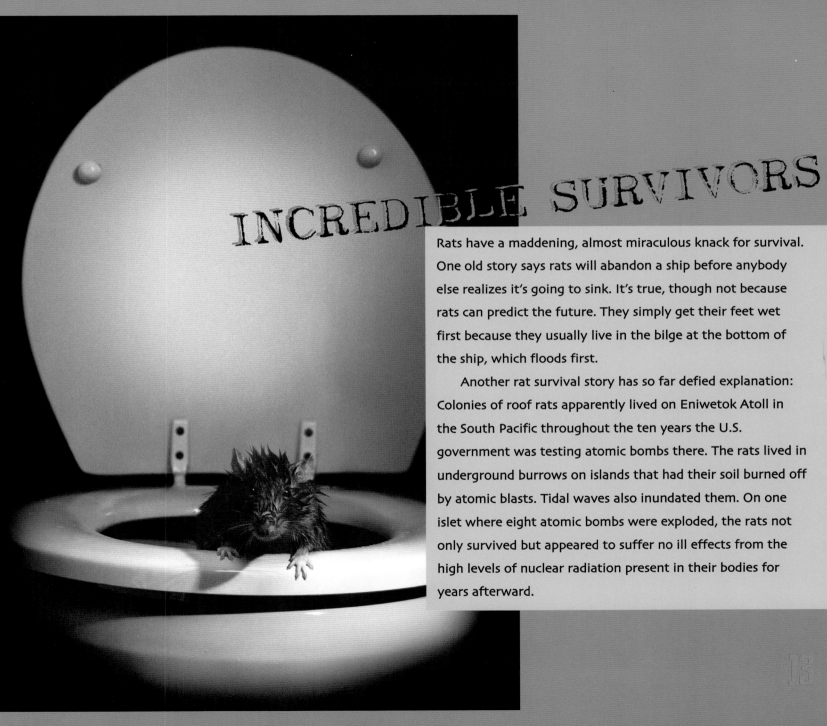

INCREDIBLE SURVIVORS

Rats have a maddening, almost miraculous knack for survival. One old story says rats will abandon a ship before anybody else realizes it's going to sink. It's true, though not because rats can predict the future. They simply get their feet wet first because they usually live in the bilge at the bottom of the ship, which floods first.

Another rat survival story has so far defied explanation: Colonies of roof rats apparently lived on Eniwetok Atoll in the South Pacific throughout the ten years the U.S. government was testing atomic bombs there. The rats lived in underground burrows on islands that had their soil burned off by atomic blasts. Tidal waves also inundated them. On one islet where eight atomic bombs were exploded, the rats not only survived but appeared to suffer no ill effects from the high levels of nuclear radiation present in their bodies for years afterward.

BEHAVIOR: ACTING LIKE RATS

Savage? Not me.

The great myth about rats is that they're savages—even to one another. In fact, rats live in colonies of up to several hundred individuals. They like to huddle together, often crawling under and over one another, or gently pushing their noses into the flanks of their companions, or grooming one another by nibbling the fur. They sleep together in a happy, ratty heap.

Rats communicate primarily by touch and scent—not language or facial expression. The members of the colony seem to recognize one another by a distinctive group odor. They also know by scent alone who's the boss, or alpha male, and they're careful to tiptoe around him.

The males of the colony defend their territory against strangers. But they generally manage to avoid violence. A resident male typically confronts a newcomer by raising his hair (to make himself look bigger) and chattering his teeth. He swaggers and threatens. As a last resort, he may even pounce on the intruder and bite him. But rats rarely fight to the death, or even to the point of serious injury.

Another big myth is that rats are filthy. In fact, rats are constantly grooming themselves. One of the first things a wild rat does on waking is lick its hands and wash its face, behind its ears, and even between its hind toes. Most humans aren't that finicky.

Rats typically move around only at night. (If you see one by day, it means lots of rats and not enough food in the neighborhood.) They travel solo, and they can range a quarter-mile or more for a meal. When a rat finds food, it will often carry the morsel in its mouth back to the nest to eat. This causes other rats to head out in search of the same food.

Rats evolved to feed on seeds and grains, but they will eat almost anything we eat. Pizza? Egg rolls? Birthday cake? Yes, *please*. Oh, and raw eggs, too.

BIG MYTH:
Rats are filthy.

"Boxing" roof rats.

Breakfast, then morning bath.

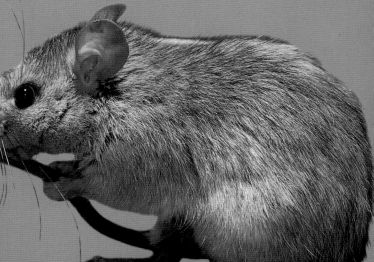

THE JOY OF RAT-WATCHING

"At three A.M. I sat alone on the concrete floor," says Stephen C. Frantz, "amused by the group of seventeen rats that had just walked across my lap." Such are the joys of being a professional rat-watcher. Frantz, a biologist for the State of New York, has traveled the world getting close to wild rats. "I'm the ever-eager student," he says, "and they're always teaching me."

So why didn't the rats attack him that night as he watched them raid a grain warehouse in India? Because Frantz was sitting in the middle of the room with plenty of escape routes all around, and he wasn't a threat.

Rats can, of course, be ferocious—but only when cornered. One time, Frantz grabbed a study rat that had gotten loose in his apartment. "It put its teeth right through my index finger. The membrane over the bone is quite sensitive, and it was grinding its teeth back and forth. I get chills thinking about it."

Another time, Frantz had the chance to bite back. He was traveling in Nepal with a group of nomads who went from farm to farm catching rats. As payment for their services, the rat-catchers got to cook up the rice the rats had stored in their burrows—plus all the rats they could eat. So did Frantz sample rat curry? "I'm a vegetarian," he says with relief. Even for a devoted rat-watcher, there is such a thing as too much joy.

Dr. Frantz in Calcutta, India.

"It put its teeth right through my index finger."

17

To test rat intelligence, scientists used to train rats to choose among levers marked with symbols, like a plus sign or a minus sign. If a rat pressed the lever with the right symbol, it got a food reward. But nature didn't build rats for pushing levers or choosing symbols. Testing them by human standards was like a bat trying to rate human intelligence by asking how well we navigate in the dark.

What if we tested rats on *their* strengths? Rats have a powerful sense of smell, and they were born to dig. So some scientists now ask rats to choose among cups of sand, each scented with a common household aroma, like cinnamon, oregano, vanilla, or chocolate. It takes the rats only one or two tries to learn that digging in oregano-scented sand, for instance, always produces a treat. (Froot Loops are a favorite.) Rats will remember a winning scent even weeks later, and they can make logical deductions about what they've learned. For instance: If sample A (the oregano) always contains the reward when it's paired with sample B (the cinnamon), but B always contains the reward when paired with C, rats are always smart enough to choose B over C, and C over D, and so on. What's the right choice when B is paired with D? Can't figure it out? A rat can.

Rats are also better than we are at navigation. Imagine a maze consisting of a hub, like the one on a bicycle wheel, and eight spokes. You're in the middle, and there's a treat at the end of each spoke. The best way for you to get all the treats with the least effort is to go down one spoke after another, in order. But a rat doesn't need to do it in order. It knows where it's been and seldom makes the mistake of going down the same spoke twice. You could say that rats have a better sense of their place in the world than we do.

So how smart are rats? It depends on how you ask the questions.

This clever rat pushes a ball up a ramp, climbs the inside of a stovepipe, and pulls a balloon down in order to gain her reward—a peanut-butter sandwich (in a blue cup).

STREET SMARTS

A curious mouse will nibble at almost any food set before it—and probably end up with its neck in a snap trap. Rats are more cautious. It takes them a night or two before they'll sample a new bait or nose around a trap—and they can taste poison in food at concentrations as low as one part per million. That's like being able to taste a teaspoonful of chocolate in 1,302 gallons of milk. If a poison sickens but does not kill them, they will remember and avoid it.

Rats even note how a new food affects fellow rats. Say a rat goes out and finds cinnamon-scented food. When it returns to the nest, other rats will smell the combination of cinnamon and carbon disulfide, a natural odor on the rat's breath. Then those rats will go out and also seek the scent of cinnamon.

MRS. RAT'S HUMBLE ABODE

Roof rats like high-rise living. They build their nests in trees, attics, and other enclosed spaces. Norway rats will also sometimes nest in the walls of a building. But they prefer to live in a hole in the ground. They typically dig their burrows no more than eighteen inches deep and stuff the central chamber with rags, bits of paper, and other kinds of nesting material to make it cozy. A system of tunnels connects different burrows.

Rats can be ingenious at finding new homes: At one sidewalk café in a downtown neighborhood, rats burrowed in the dirt in the handsome, table-high planters. Customers savoring their chocolate croissants never noticed the rat burrows visible under the yew bushes, right at the backs of their necks.

Even in the very best backyards, rats often nest unsuspected within a few feet of a garbage shed, a bird feeder, or a well-stocked bowl of dog food. At the White House a few years ago, the ground under the azalea bushes by the service entrance was pockmarked with rat burrows. The president's household staff was using an open truck to store garbage then, and it was heaven for rats. At times, rats have even turned up behind the file cabinets inside the White House itself. Nowadays, the White House uses a ratproof hydraulic trash container, and like everybody else with an occasional rat problem, the president would rather not discuss it.

The moral is that you may have the best security system in the world, but rats can still sneak in. In fact, brand-new buildings often have them— even, in one case, on the fifty-second floor of a new skyscraper. Construction workers can be careless with their food, so rats come for lunch and end up staying, getting built into the new walls.

A Norway rat peeking out of its burrow.

At times, rats have even turned up behind the file cabinets inside the White House itself.

Beginning in 1347, a terrible plague swept out of Asia and across Europe, killing millions of people. Nobody knew the cause, but the symptoms were sudden and deadly: first shivering and weakness, then headache, chills, slurred speech, confusion, and painful swelling of the limbs. Soon the nervous system collapsed. After four or five days, the victim's skin began turning black.

Many people blamed the epidemic on foul air and walked around sniffing flowers (or "posies") for protection. Some people believe this is the origin of the rhyme children still recite: "Ring around the rosy, a pocket full of posies. Ashes, ashes. We all fall down."

By the end of the fourteenth century, the "Black Death," or bubonic plague, had taken a third of the population of Europe, and it came back repeatedly for centuries afterward. But it wasn't until the 1890s that researchers recognized the true cause: Fleas bit roof rats and picked up bacteria in their blood. When these same fleas made the leap to human hosts and bit them, too, they transmitted the bacteria.

A 14th-century Bible depicted victims of plague.

The rat flea (shown greatly enlarged) specializes in clinging to rat fur but can bite humans, too.

TOO MANY RATS?

According to popular wisdom, the average city has one rat per person. This statistic gets repeated ritually in newspaper articles about rats. But it's a myth. It dates from a survey sent to residents in rural, not urban, areas in England in 1908. The survey asked farmers to estimate their rat population, and they guessed that one rat per acre sounded about right. At the time, the local human population was about one person per acre. And thus the one-rat-per-person myth was born. Almost a century later, people still insist that New York City, with 8 million people, must also have 8 million rats.

But it isn't so. In fact, the only good scientific study of rat populations in this country took place in 1949 and found one rat for every thirty-six people in New York City and one for every fifteen in Baltimore. Nobody ever cites these figures because, as one exterminator put it, "It doesn't hurt to have people thinking there are more rats out there than there really are."

So how many rats do you really have in your town? Here is a reliable, scientific estimate: too many.

Could rats *still* cause an outbreak of plague? In fact, an epidemic occurred in India just a few years ago, and less than a century ago plague killed 10 million people there. But the three factors needed for an epidemic—many fleas, many rodents, and the disease organism itself—rarely coincide in one place. So plague is now uncommon. In the United States, a few cases occur each year in the western states, usually among people who have actually handled rodents. If victims get to the doctor soon enough, plague is relatively easy to treat with antibiotics.

Rats also get blamed for a long list of other illnesses, including rat-borne typhus, leptospirosis, salmonellosis, shigellosis, trichinosis, and rat-bite fever. But it's unclear how often rats actually cause sickness. For instance, most cases of the food poisoning known as salmonellosis are due not to rats but to our own unsanitary food-handling practices.

A more serious problem is that rats bite thousands of Americans a year. But dogs bite 3 *million* of us each year, and their bite, unlike the rat's, carries a significant risk of rabies. A rat bite normally requires the same treatment as any ordinary puncture wound. The U.S. government has concluded that rats do not constitute a public-health problem in this country.

Even so, as one rat-control official puts it, "Rats cause a lot of psychological stress. There's a fear factor that's unlike anything else."

To test a sewer rat's fleas for plague, biologists in Madagascar blow on the rodent and suck up the falling insects with a vacuum tube.

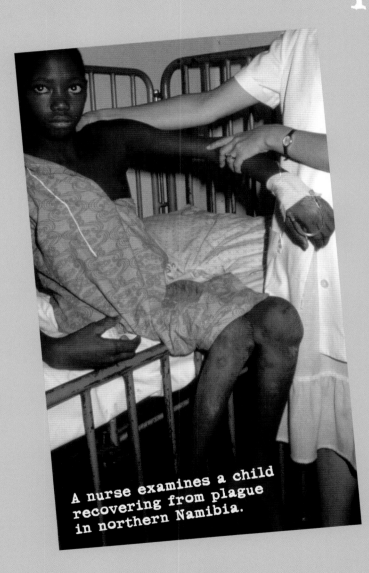

A nurse examines a child recovering from plague in northern Namibia.

"There's a fear factor that's unlike anything else."

An oil-rich sheikh in Abu Dhabi used to store his cash in closets and boxes—until he discovered that rats had eaten $2 million of it. But that was pocket change compared with the damage rats do worldwide.

People's homes sometimes burn down because rats have gnawed the insulation off electrical wires. Rats also steal or spoil huge amounts of food meant for humans.

A single rat eats twenty or more pounds of food a year. But rats seldom occur singly. One researcher studying a small grain warehouse in Calcutta, India, found that it had about two hundred rats—and that they ate enough rice to feed eleven people for a year (not counting what they damaged with their urine and droppings). Add up the number of grain warehouses and the number of rats in poor countries around the world, and the damage quickly translates into hunger and sometimes even starvation for millions of people.

Rats also contribute to environmental damage. Because rats eat their crops, farmers have to cut down more forests and plant more fields to feed their families. In one study in the state of Penang in Malaysia, researchers found that reducing the rat population saved $365,000 worth of rice in a single season. To grow that much extra rice, local farmers would have needed 1,200 acres of land.

A single rat
eats twenty or
more pounds of
food a year.

The human war against rats is a catalog of interesting ideas gone wrong. In Bombay, India, for instance, municipal authorities once required rat-control workers to deliver a quota of dead rats every night. So one enterprising worker actually raised rats at home to help meet his quota. In Indonesia, a local government decreed that couples could marry only after they paid a license fee of ten rats. To get a divorce took twenty-three rats.

Another bright idea was to enlist natural predators in the great war on rats. When roof rats nibbled their sugar cane stalks, farmers in Hawaii and the West Indies introduced the mongoose, a ferocious killer back home in Africa and India. Unfortunately, rats feed by night, mongooses by day. So the newcomers turned their hunger on local birds and reptiles, driving some native species to extinction. The rats continued to frolic in the sugar cane.

You'd think that humans would have done the right thing when it came to cats. The ancient Egyptians revered cats as rat killers (though even a very ratty cat will typically catch no more than twenty-five or so a year). But some Europeans blamed cats, not rats, for the Black Death. In one of the great cases of mistaken identity on record, the English alone destroyed two hundred thousand cats during the Great Plague of 1665.

A rat killer in Bombay with a day's haul.

Barn owl with rat snack.

SUPER RATS

In the 1950s, researchers developed new rat poisons using anticoagulants, which thin the blood. When a large-enough dose accumulates in a rat's body, it bleeds to death internally. But rats in some areas developed resistance to anticoagulants. It was evolution in action: The poisons killed the most vulnerable rats. The least vulnerable rats survived to reproduce and spread their natural resistance through the population.

In areas with these "super rats," anticoagulants are no longer effective. But they may indirectly kill some of the rat's natural enemies: Anticoagulants routinely turn up in barn owls and other predators that have been poisoned by eating rats.

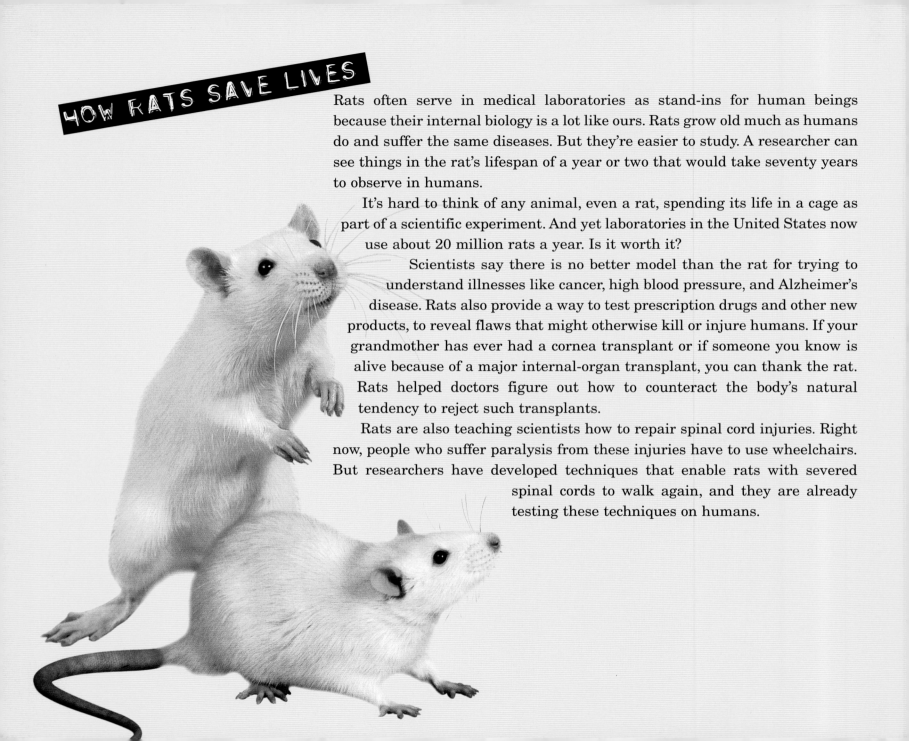

HOW RATS SAVE LIVES

Rats often serve in medical laboratories as stand-ins for human beings because their internal biology is a lot like ours. Rats grow old much as humans do and suffer the same diseases. But they're easier to study. A researcher can see things in the rat's lifespan of a year or two that would take seventy years to observe in humans.

It's hard to think of any animal, even a rat, spending its life in a cage as part of a scientific experiment. And yet laboratories in the United States now use about 20 million rats a year. Is it worth it?

Scientists say there is no better model than the rat for trying to understand illnesses like cancer, high blood pressure, and Alzheimer's disease. Rats also provide a way to test prescription drugs and other new products, to reveal flaws that might otherwise kill or injure humans. If your grandmother has ever had a cornea transplant or if someone you know is alive because of a major internal-organ transplant, you can thank the rat. Rats helped doctors figure out how to counteract the body's natural tendency to reject such transplants.

Rats are also teaching scientists how to repair spinal cord injuries. Right now, people who suffer paralysis from these injuries have to use wheelchairs. But researchers have developed techniques that enable rats with severed spinal cords to walk again, and they are already testing these techniques on humans.

In this study, a rat serves as a model for how the body metabolizes sugar.

SPACE RATS

On August 20, 1960, two rats (and a small menagerie of other animals) aboard the Russian spacecraft *Sputnik II* became the first living creatures to return to Earth from orbit in outer space. Once rats had boldly gone where no man had gone before, it was safe for human space travelers to follow. Rats have continued to travel into space for experiments ever since. On one NASA space shuttle flight in the 1990s, for instance, rats provided remarkable new evidence about how the body adjusts to weightlessness. Rats, like humans, get their sense of balance from the inner ear. But in space, the inner ear sends weaker signals. So the weightless rats actually added new nerve cells in the brain to amplify signals from the ear. It was the first time anyone realized that the adult brain can grow new cells.

Kady Carson, a twelve-year-old in Newport Beach, California, sleeps with eleven rats in her bedroom. Sometimes when she's watching television, one of them snuggles up on her shoulder and falls asleep under her hair. "Some of my friends think I'm really weird," she says. "They think a normal pet is a cat or a dog. But I think pet rats are neat."

Her rats have names like Pixie and Dixie, and they come in colors from black-and-white to beige-capped to blue. They're descended from lab rats, not wild rats. Kady keeps them in special two- and three-story cages, and the rats like it if she rigs up a hammock for them from an old T-shirt. They also like to come out once a day to sit on her lap or climb on a shoulder. "They're smart," Kady says. "I can teach them their names and they'll come when I call." She feeds them pellet food from the pet store. But they also like Cheerios, bananas, or almost anything else.

People who keep rats sometimes enter them in beauty contests sponsored by the American Fancy Rat and Mouse Association. Judges like a rat to be "long and somewhat racy in appearance." They'll mark down a rat if its eyes lack "animation and interest."

But Kady belongs to another group, the Rat & Mouse Club of America, which just likes rats to be nice. So it holds competitions in categories like "longest tail" or "best lap loafer" or "most active lap rat." There's also a rat agility course, like the one dogs compete on, with a mini teeter-totter, a tunnel, a ladder to climb, a platform, and, for the really ambitious rat, a bell to ring.

Darwin, a hairless rat.

A black-hooded rat.

People who keep rats sometimes enter them in beauty contests.

A beige Dumbo rat.

Rats have crept into our myths and dreams, as well as into our houses. In the folktale of the Pied Piper, for instance, rats infested the medieval German town of Hamelin. "They fought the dogs and killed the cats . . . and ate the cheeses out of the vats," wrote Robert Browning. A man dressed in pied (or multicolored) clothes came and lured the rats away with his pipe music. But local officials wouldn't pay his fee, so he lured away the town's children, too. That's the story, anyway. It could be that the children really disappeared because they died of plague after collecting rats killed by a visiting *Rattenfänger,* or rat catcher. No one knows for sure.

Rats sometimes turn up as likable rogues in popular books or movies, like Kenneth Grahame's *The Wind in the Willows.* But mostly they represent evil incarnate. We say, "I smell a rat" when we think something's wrong or "you dirty rat" when someone is wicked. To betray friends is to "rat on" them.

But in one Hindu temple in Rajasthan, India, worshipers believe that rats are the reincarnated souls of mystics or saints. More than four thousand rats live in the temple. Worshipers go barefoot, and custom holds that if you step on a rat and kill it, you must pay its weight in silver or gold. Stepping on rat droppings, on the other hand, is free.

In the evening, ceremonial drums and bells call forth the rats. The priests present a dish of rice the size of a basketball, which is instantly swarming with rats. When the rice is almost gone, a priest retrieves the dish and passes it around so the members of the congregation can each take a few grains of leftover rice to eat.

Whatever myths we choose to impose on them, rats are neither saints nor demons. They are merely animals—sometimes good, sometimes bad. Ugly? Well, maybe so. But wherever they happen to appear, rats are *always* interesting.

YEEEK! IT'S DINNER.

Rats dine nightly at this temple in Rajasthan, India.

One way to control rats would be to have them for dinner. With ketchup, say. Or maybe *rats au poivre*. The rats on a British warship once did so much damage to the regular food that the sailors ate the rats instead and came to regard rat pie as "a great delicacy." Food markets in the Philippines used to offer barbecued rats, and in Sicily they sold them in ropes, tied by the tails like onions. The Chinese like them dried and split. "Rats used as food stop the hair from falling out," one believer wrote, "and make the locks soft, silky, and beautiful."

Rats for sale in Luang Prebang market, Laos.

But eating rats is not just a matter of distant times and places. As part of a rat control study, U.S. government researchers once took four hundred rats and some pork and made sausages in four distinct combinations. The 50-50 rat-pork combo was everybody's favorite.

In fact, despite our best efforts, rat is part of our daily diet: A rat sheds a million hairs a year. It's impossible to keep farm produce completely free of rats and mice, so the U.S. government sets a maximum allowable amount of rodent hairs and droppings in processed foods like peanut butter. Lunch, anyone?

iNDeX

Text copyright © 2002 by Richard Conniff
Front cover photograph copyright © Grove Pashley
Back cover photograph copyright © Peter Samuels/Getty Images

Photograph Credits (clockwise from top to bottom or left to right as appropriate):
Endpapers: © Grove Pashley. Title page: all photos © Grove Pashley. Page 6: © OSF/Jim Frazier/Mantis/Animals Animals; © Carolyn A. McKeone/Photo Researchers. Page 7: © Stephen Dalton/Photo Researchers. Page 8: © Stephen Dalton/Animals Animals. Page 9: © Stephen Dalton/Animals Animals; © Tom McHugh/Photo Researchers. Page 10: © David Sams/Getty Images. Page 11: all photos © Grove Pashley. Page 12: © OSF/R. Redfern/Animals Animals; © Stephen Dalton/Photo Researchers. Page 13: © Grove Pashley. Page 14: © Tom McHugh/Photo Researchers; © Grove Pashley. Page 15: © OSF/J. Downer/Animals Animals; © Stephen Dalton/Photo Researchers; © Tom McHugh/Photo Researchers. Page 16: Courtesy of Stephen C. Frantz. Page 17: Courtesy of Stephen C. Frantz. Page 18: © James L. Stanfield/National Geographic Image Collection. Page 19: © Peter Samuels/Getty Images; © Grove Pashley. Page 20: © Terry Whittaker/Photo Researchers. Page 21: © OSF/M. Hamblin/Animals Animals; © Grove Pashley; © Terry Whittaker/Photo Researchers. Page 22: © Bettmann/Corbis; © Dr. Tony Brain/Photo Researchers; © Grove Pashley. Page 23: © Grove Pashley. Page 24: © Nicole Duplaix/Corbis. Page 25: © Nicole Duplaix/Corbis; © Grove Pashley. Page 26: © Grove Pashley; © Tom McHugh/Photo Researchers. Page 27: © John Downer/Getty Images; © Holt Studios/Nigel Cattlin/Photo Researchers. Page 28: © Jeffrey L. Rotman/Corbis. Page 29: © Grove Pashley; © Grove Pashley; © Gallo Images/Corbis. Page 30: © Holt Studios/Nigel Cattlin/Photo Researchers; copyright-free. Page 31: © Richard T. Nowitz/Corbis. Page 32: © Grove Pashley. Page 33: all photos © Carolyn A. McKeone/Photo Researchers. Page 34: © Bettmann/Corbis; © Grove Pashley. Page 35: © James L. Stanfield/National Geographic Image Collection; © Christophe Loviny/Corbis. Page 36: all photos © Grove Pashley. Page 37: © Grove Pashley.

Published by Crown Publishers, an imprint of Random House Children's Books, a division of Random House, Inc., 1540 Broadway, New York, NY 10036.

CROWN and colophon are trademarks of Random House, Inc.
www.randomhouse.com/kids

Library of Congress Cataloging-in-Publication Data
Conniff, Richard, 1951–
Rats! : the good, the bad, and the ugly / by Richard Conniff.
                        p.   cm.
Summary: Discusses the physical characteristics, behavior, origins, various types, interaction with humans, and more, of rats.
ISBN 0-375-81207-5 (trade) — ISBN 0-375-91207-X (lib. bdg.)
1. Rats—Juvenile literature. [1. Rats.] I. Title.
QL737.R666 C65   2002
599.35'2—dc21   2002067355

PRINTED in HONG KONG
November 2002
10 9 8 7 6 5 4 3 2 1
First Edition